HOME GUARDS INFANTRY TRAINING

— HOW TO FIGHT —

The Naval & Military Press Ltd

Published by

The Naval & Military Press Ltd
Unit 5 Riverside, Brambleside
Bellbrook Industrial Estate
Uckfield, East Sussex
TN22 1QQ England

Tel: +44 (0)1825 749494

www.naval-military-press.com
www.nmarchive.com

In reprinting in facsimile from the original, any imperfections are inevitably reproduced and the quality may fall short of modern type and cartographic standards.

PREFACE

ANY German attempt at invasion must fail if the defending forces show a determined resistance. The present battle is a clash between two faiths, the German faith in their military superiority and the British faith in the freedom of mankind. Our opponents are completely regimented, they are disciplined from childhood, and that is the weak spot in their armour. We are left to work out our own lives with the minimum of authority, and this has encouraged individual initiative in our character.

This individualism makes the Britisher superior to the German, especially when things are going strictly to plan. Wisely enough the Authorities have not tried to organise the Home Guard on the strict Army basis. But nevertheless, some discipline is essential. The small amount of drilling which units have had so far has not been given with the idea of making parade ground automatons. Drill is essential if bodies of men are to be moved quickly and orderly from one spot to another. Home Guardsmen themselves are getting enthusiastic about their soldierly bearing and this is one of the most promising signs of their determination to do this job properly.

Let discipline come from within the group and not be forced from outside. When gathering at Headquarters for a parade don't hang about in groups outside the building. Fall into columns of three and dress off correctly. Don't wait to be told every time. Help your leaders and your instructors. Get to know the members of your platoon and fall in together.

The more you do for yourself the quicker can the instructor get on to the real training. That means more time for tactical exercises, lectures and scheming.

Instructors are scarce. If you wait to be told everything the organisers will be hard pressed to find the necessary men, and there is a danger that some may be chosen who, although keen and willing, have not that experience of modern conditions which is essential. We cannot afford to have obsolete ideas impressed on this new army. Here again it is up to the individual.

The subjects dealt with in this book have been treated in a general way, on the lines of elementary tactics, with the hope that this method will help the individual to become much more than a mere cog in an excellent military machine.

Appreciation is due to the band of realists who have organised the Osterley Park Training Camp, for the encouragement and advice received. It is thanks to such help that this book has been made possible.

Readers must not take the contents as a description of hard and fast rules, but should consider them as a series of suggestions to be weighed in the balance of their own circumstances and experience. If they are thereby encouraged to develop new ideas, my purpose has been fully served.

For guidance on the subjects of Scouting and Stalking, Guerrilla Tactics, Camouflage and the Manufacture of Bombs (omitted from this book through shortage of space) readers must look elsewhere.

So read all you can, buy as many books as possible on the various subjects which a good soldier must know. Use your Public Libraries, buy the excellent publications of His Majesty's Stationery Office, etc. Find out for yourself, don't wait to be told ; then show Hitler, indeed show the World, what British amateurs can do.

Coventry, September, 1940.   FREDERIC PILLING.

INTRODUCTION

German Tactics

BEFORE dealing in detail with the recommended training, it is well to consider the characteristics and tactics of the enemy, since these determine the type of action—and support the drastic measures—which are advised.

German forces are extremely well led and organised. All fighting is carried out ruthlessly. Only one law of warfare is recognised—success in the particular operation. Sacrifice of German forces is not counted as long as the action gives the planned result. In addition, captured territory is deliberately terrorised by the massacre of inhabitants chosen at random, including men, women and children of all ages. Prisoners and women and children are used as cover for the advancing troops, while refugees become part of the scheme for disorganising the defenders.

Efficient opposition must be equally ruthless and the British respect for person and property does not fit in with the new conditions. This enemy must be *destroyed* at all costs. Should this call for a parallel destruction of British property, whether individual or national, and even of British lives, there must be no hesitation in facing the situation. We simply cannot afford to give the invader a military advantage in the hope of saving some treasured possession. He will probably destroy it in any case when it has served his purpose.

German strategy is based on the theories of the famous Clausewitz. In recent operations the tactics have comprised simultaneous attacks with armoured forces at several points, these acting as steel fingers probing the strength of the defenders. Then follows an immediate concentration, so easy with aircraft and mechanised troops, at the one spot where the advance has made most progress. A similar scheme is almost certain to be adopted for an invasion of this country. Attacks will be made at many points around the coast and at important centres inland. Bombing aircraft will act as long range artillery, laying a destructive barrage. Parachute troops will attack vital centres and landing grounds, not necessarily aerodromes. Air borne troops will deploy on the latter, and should any one area prove easy to overrun the full German attack would be aimed there.

The capture of so much Allied equipment during the Flanders operations will be turned to good account and British uniforms and planes will certainly be used. Police and post office uniforms must be expected when parachute troops land. The British people are law-abiding and usually follow police instructions in a good humoured way. Bringing psychology to his aid, the German realises the great opportunity this gives for the issue of false instructions. The local police must therefore be well known to the members of all services operating during an invasion. The postman's bag is such a handy store for grenades and explosives that postmen too should be known to the defenders. In some towns the police and Home Guard have been paraded together for this purpose.

Examples of ruthless tricks are given below, and these are typical of the actions to be expected from German troops.

Parachute troops on landing often surrender immediately. They stand with arms raised crying " Kamerad " or " I surrender." But their fists are closed and each hand conceals an egg bomb. Anyone approaching to take them prisoner is in extreme danger.

An alternative to the above is to have one or two parachutists armed with " Tommy " guns lying hidden nearby while those standing to surrender act as decoys.

To overcome these two tricks always keep under cover,

or lie down in open country, and make the enemy walk towards you with arms outstretched and fingers held wide to expose the palms. Be ready to shoot at the first sign of treachery.

Private cars and motor cycles are commandeered and German troops often wear civilian clothes or the uniforms of the opposing forces.

As soon as Brussels was occupied, private cars with women drivers were rounded up and filled with German officers and men. These took hats from civilians near by and were immediately sent forward to contact the British. Our men mistook them for refugees and, when the Germans dismounted and opened fire, hesitated to return fire because of the women drivers. Eventually they were forced to shoot, and some of the women were hit, but not before British casualties had occurred. The chivalry of our men did not save the women but gave an immediate advantage to the Germans. Such risks cannot be taken since the slightest weakness encourages a terrific concentration of enemy strength.

Great use is made of noise to demoralise untrained forces and refugees in order to upset the operations of regular troops. Only experience can counteract these tactics, but if everyone keeps busy during attacks, especially of aircraft, there is less tendency to be overawed.

Light tanks of about eight tons weight were transported by air during the Russian occupation of Bessarabia. A repetition of this must be expected so that light armoured forces comprising two or three tanks and an advance party of motor cyclists on commandeered machines are very possible opponents. Remember that tanks will always endeavour to outflank a defensive position and attack it from the rear.

Prisoners of war and civilians of all ages and both sexes are shot at random just to overawe the inhabitants of occupied territory. No terror or injustice is neglected if it will help to impress the conquered people of the superiority of German strength.

The Germans are prepared to lose three quarters of their forces if the remainder can gain the objective. There can be no doubt of the fanatical enthusiasm of the young German soldiers. Fed by the overwhelming propaganda of the Nazi system these men willingly sacrifice themselves to a cause which the free peoples of the world recognise as a threat to civilisation itself. There is no cowardice about the German army as a whole. It is simply one vast machine designed to blot out everything in its path. But, like all man-made things, it has its weakness, and that weakness will be plain when the Nazi system meets the determined but loosely organised resistance of the *entire* people of these Islands.

Four main phases mark the latest German technique. First, strong traitorous activity; second, the use of parachute troops to gain control of suitable landing grounds. These areas need not be aerodromes as there are innumerable open spaces in this country suitable for their purpose. Then follows the actual landing of air borne troops. The fourth phase is the use of bombing aircraft as long range artillery to smash any strong opposition which is holding up an advance.

Another possibility is the use of captured British aircraft to transport German troops in British uniforms to aerodromes where the same type of aircraft is stationed. And they have long range artillery across the English Channel. The Germans have developed suitable guns with a range of 30 miles and may try to cut off a pocket of the country around Dover so as to gain a port for the disembarkation of troops, tanks and supplies. Aircraft would certainly be used to spread a barrage beyond this area and disorganise the defence.

These are, at the time of writing, mere surmises, but they are factors for which the Home Guard must be prepared.

CHAPTER I

Elementary Training

MODERN armies depend much more on the individual soldier than did those of other wars. Training nowadays is organised to bring out the initiative of each man. Even squad drill, which at one time was considered mainly as an exercise in obedience, is now treated as exercise in manœuvreability. The soldier must realise that precision in drill will enable a body of men to move rapidly with the minimum of effort.

The following details of Squad Drill without arms are the foundation of military formations.

Starting with the individual. Slovenly drill is definitely harmful, and every movement must be made smartly *and quietly*. On no account should the feet be stamped on the ground when coming to attention, halting or turning.

The ATTENTION position is not a stiff, unnatural stance but simply, as its name implies, one of alertness, in preparation for orders. Heels must be together and in line, with feet turned outwards at angle of 30 degrees. The body should be erect and balanced comfortably on both feet. Do not strain the chest or shoulders, and hold the head evenly with chin slightly back. Eyes look straight forward. Both arms should hang naturally from the shoulders with the wrists straight and hands closed. Do not clench hands, this would cause fatigue; let the backs of the fingers touch the trousers and point the thumbs downwards holding them just at the trouser seams. Breathe naturally and avoid unnecessary strain. It is possible to hold this position for long periods without effort, keeping the mind ready for any commands.

With the order STAND AT EASE move the left foot 12 inches to the left, and distribute the weight of the body evenly on both feet.

Simultaneously with this movement bring both hands behind the back and hold the right hand in the left. If, however, the command is given in *marching order* but when rifles are not being carried, the arms remain at the sides as at attention.

In the stand at ease position a relaxation is ordered by STAND—EASY. This does not mean complete freedom to lounge and move at will. The body and arms may be turned as required but on no account must the feet be moved as this would upset the formation of the squad. At the cautionary command " Squad " the correct stand at ease position is resumed.

These are the three basic positions for drill and from the first all further movements are carried out. Remember that in all commands a caution is given first and any manœuvre must be carried out on the final word of the order.

Where the command is given in one word, such as " ATTENTION," the order will be: " SQUAD (or Company or Parade)—'TION." Where the command is in two words there will be a pause between them, for example, " QUICK—MARCH," the dash denoting the pause in command. In addition in early training a complete instruction of the intended movement precedes the actual command; for instance: " Squad will advance— QUICK—MARCH." Wait for the last word of all commands.

Simple turns are made in two movements from the attention position:—

(*a*) On the command, " RIGHT--TURN ":

Keeping the body erect, swing to the right on the right heel and left toe. At the end of the 90 degree turn put the right foot flat on the ground, carrying the whole weight of the body on the right leg, and keep the left heel raised.

After a slight pause the second movement, bringing the left foot smartly to the right foot, completes the manœuvre, and the body is again at " attention."

(b) On the command, " LEFT—TURN ":

The movements are as above but the instructions RIGHT and LEFT are reversed.

(c) On the command, " RIGHT ABOUT—TURN ":

The first movement is carried out exactly as for right turn, except that the body is turned through 180 degrees instead of 90 degrees.

The second movement is identical with that for the right turn.

(d) On the command, " LEFT ABOUT—TURN ":

Reverse procedure for the right about turn.

(e) On the command, "RIGHT (or left) IN—CLINE":

Inclining is turning to right or left through an angle of 45 degrees instead of the 90 degrees of the normal right or left turn. The two movements for this order are similar to those for the turns.

During all the above movements the arms must be kept close to the sides as in the attention position.

The true test of the quality of elementary training is marching, and concentration on this will be amply repaid.

Leg movements must be natural and at each swing the knee should be bent just enough for the foot to clear the ground. Keep the head and body erect, arms straight with hands closed comfortably, thumbs forward, and swing each arm well forward in time with the opposite leg, for the quick march. For the slow march the arms are kept at the sides. Both feet must point forward, avoid turning the toes outwards.

The correct forward pace is 30 inches long and in a *quick march* there are 120 paces to the minute. These cover 100 yards. *Slow march* is at 70 paces per minute, and in *double time* 180 paces a minute give 200 yards distance.

When drilling in formation it is often necessary to " step

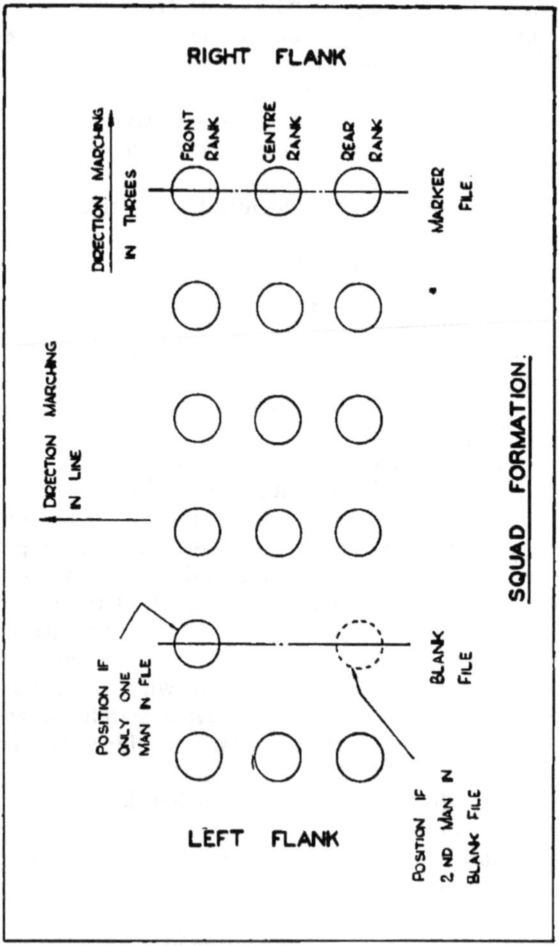
RIGHT FLANK
DIRECTION MARCHING IN THREES
FRONT RANK
CENTRE RANK
REAR RANK
MARKER FILE
DIRECTION MARCHING IN LINE
POSITION IF ONLY ONE MAN IN FILE
BLANK FILE
POSITION IF 2 ND MAN IN BLANK FILE
LEFT FLANK
SQUAD FORMATION.

FIG. 1

out " or " step short." In the former the pace is increased to 33 inches length and in the latter reduced to 21 inches. In *double time* the stepping out pace is 40 inches.

A normal side pace is 12 inches, but when moving to " cover off " a front rank man a pace of 24 inches is taken in " dressing " to speed up the action.

So much for the individual actions. Now turn to collective drill. A small body of men undergoing instruction is called a " squad " and this word precedes all orders. In more formal drill the words " platoon," " company " or " parade " will be used, depending on the number of men involved.

Before drilling, soldiers must *fall in*. This means forming three *ranks* or lines, and these are one pace, or 30 inches, apart. The right hand man of each rank is the " marker," and these three take up their positions first. The remainder then fall in on the left of the markers. Front rank men except the marker get the correct *dressing* by looking over the right shoulder, extending the right arm with hand clenched so that the knuckles touch the shoulder of the man to the right. When the dressing is correct the rank should be a perfectly straight line, each man standing with body erect, head turned to right and right arm extended. The command for this action is " RIGHT—DRESS." Each man in the second and third ranks moves sideways to *cover off* the front rank man, that is to get in line behind him, at the same time looking to the right to line up with the marker at the end of each rank. Only front rank men extend their right arms, but all men look to the right, and each should just be able to see the lower part of the face of the man next but one to him.

When rifles are carried, the *dressing* is obtained by raising the left arm and not the right one. Alignment, however, is still by turning the head to the right unless the command is given " LEFT—DRESS " in which case the man at the left hand end (or left flank) of the rank becomes the marker.

If the number of men in the squad is not a multiple of three, one file, that is one of the lines running from front to rear of the formation, will be a *blank file*. This incomplete file is always arranged at the second from the left flank of the formation. If there are only two men in this file, e.g. in a squad of 17 men, the centre rank is left empty. With a squad of 16 men, giving only one man in the blank file, he takes up position in the front rank as shown in fig. 1.

On ceremonial parades the right—dress attitude will be held until the command " EYES—FRONT " when all ranks will turn their heads smartly to the front, eyes looking straight ahead. On all other occasions each man will turn his head as soon as he is in correct position and, without any instruction or command, stand at attention ready for the next order.

This may be "SQUAD, STAND AT—EASE," followed by " STAND—EASY." Note the preliminary caution, " SQUAD," and the pause in the actual command. Move only on the last word.

When drill is to commence the command will be " SQUAD " (or " company " or " parade ") at which everyone will come to the *stand at ease* position. This is followed by " SQUAD—'TION."

With the command " SQUAD—NUMBER," the right hand man in the front rank calls " ONE," the next man " TWO " and so on from the right to the left of the line. Infantry formations do not turn the head to the left when numbering. Look straight to the front.

Should an inspection of the ranks be required the order " OPEN ORDER—MARCH " is given. On the word " MARCH " the front rank steps forward two paces and the rear rank back two paces, coming to attention again. After the inspection the command will be " CLOSE ORDER—MARCH," when the front rank moves two paces back and the rear two paces forward. Alignment should be corrected after each movement unless the drill is under ceremonial conditions when dressing is always by command.

When the entire body of men has to move the command is " THE SQUAD WILL ADVANCE (preliminary instruction) BY THE RIGHT (direction for maintaining alignment), QUICK (cautionary pause) MARCH." The instruction for alignment may be given as " BY THE LEFT " in which case dressings are taken from the left.

At the word " MARCH " (*see* fig. 2) the whole body of men step off with the left foot, the men in each rank glancing occasionally to the right to maintain the alignment while the right hand man in the front rank chooses a point in the distance straight ahead and one nearer in the same line to sight his advance and so keep to a direct course. This is important as the advance of the whole squad depends on this man. There must be correct pace-length and dressing if the movement is to be executed neatly.

At the command " SQUAD—HALT," which will be given in the quick march as the right foot is coming forward, a normal pace is taken with the left foot and the right brought up to it, the right hand being brought smartly to the side at the same time.

Instead of halting the squad the command " MARK—TIME " may be given. The foot then moving completes a pace and then the feet are lifted alternately about six inches from the ground keeping the time as in marching. The arms are kept steady at the sides and the body erect.

This may be followed by the order " HALT," or if forward movement has to be resumed the command is " FOR—WARD." The men then step off with the left foot as in the original " quick—march " order, again paying strict attention to pace-length and dressing.

When marching (*see* fig. 2), on the command "ABOUT—TURN "complete a pace with the right foot, begin the turn with the left foot, then lift the right foot, turn the

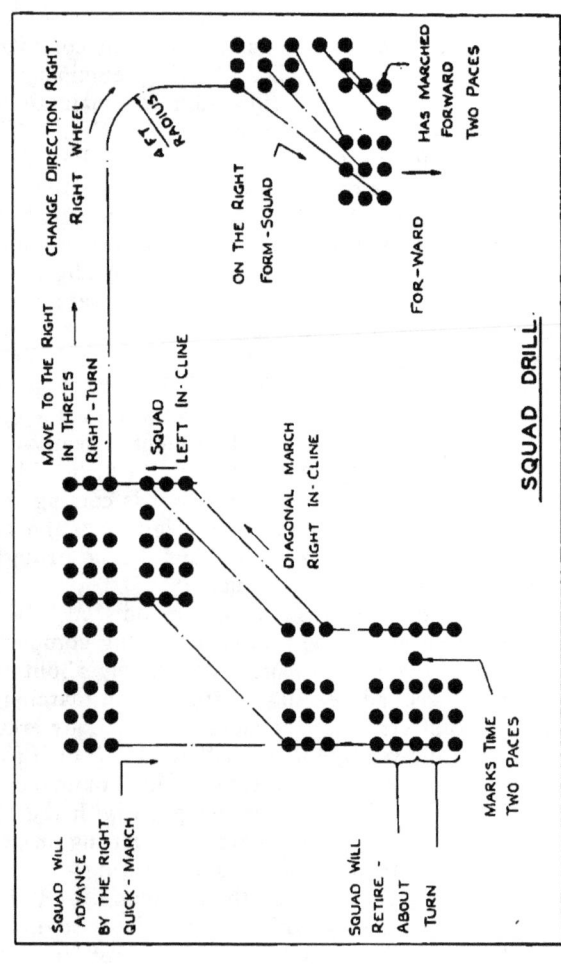

Fig. 2

body to the new direction, put the right foot down on the spot from which it was lifted, and bring the left foot beside it. This gives a sequence of three beats, and with the turn completed step off, still keeping time, with the right foot in a normal pace.

The command "ABOUT—TURN" will be prefaced by a preliminary instruction: "THE SQUAD WILL RETIRE (pause), ABOUT (pause) TURN." Where a blank file has only one man, i.e. in the front rank, he will, *when marching in line* (*see* fig. 1), mark time for two paces on the word " ABOUT." This will bring him into line with the rear rank which when the turn is completed becomes the front rank in the new direction of march. The blank file is therefore kept in order and the front rank always complete.

If on completion of this movement the squad is only required to fall back a short distance, the manœuvre will be repeated on this command: " THE SQUAD WILL ADVANCE—ABOUT—TURN."

The next movement shown in fig. 2 is on the command, " DIAGONAL MARCH—RIGHT IN—CLINE." On the syllable " CLINE " each man turns half right and marches in the new direction. The squad keeps the same formation as in the previous order.

When the required position has been reached, and if the squad has to continue in the direction previous to the incline the command will be, " THE SQUAD WILL RETIRE (or advance, depending on the original direction)— LEFT IN—CLINE." At this every man turn half left and the squad marches forward in line.

To make a quick turn the command is: " MOVE TO THE RIGHT IN THREES—RIGHT—TURN." The left foot is then brought to just in front of the right. A turn is made using the left foot as a pivot and the advance in the new direction is started with the right foot at normal pace. If the order is for a *left turn* in the above instructions right and left are reversed. So that the turn to the left is made on the right foot.

An alternative method to the *incline* changing direction is the *wheel*. This order preceded by a preliminary instruction thus: "CHANGE DIRECTION RIGHT (or left), RIGHT (or left)—WHEEL." The inner man of the leading three will turn on a four feet radius for a quarter circle, stepping short (21-inch pace). The centre man follows round at normal pace (30 inches) while the outer man steps out (33-inch pace). The arms are kept at the sides during this movement. Succeeding threes repeat these steps as they reach the point at which the manœuvre commenced.

If the squad is halted or told to mark time before the wheel is completed the threes which have not changed direction will cover off on the others as quickly as possible, taking the shortest route. The order is: "REAR FILES—COVER."

To extend the front of a file formation and keep the movement in the same direction the command is: "ON THE RIGHT FORM—SQUAD." The right hand man of the leading three carries straight on for two paces and marks time. The remainder right incline and march into line with the first man, covering off from the left flank, into three ranks and marking time as they get into position (*see* fig. 2).

At the command "FOR—WARD" the squad marches on in its original direction.

For an order "ON THE LEFT FORM—SQUAD" the above instructions are reversed as to right and left.

If the command "AT THE HALT" precedes "ON THE RIGHT FORM—SQUAD" the leading man marches two paces and halts and the rest halt and dress off as they reach position in the new formation.

At the end of the drill the order will be: "SQUAD DIS—MISS." If an officer is in charge of the party, the men make a right turn, look straight ahead and salute. After a pause equal to four paces at quick march, the squad breaks up quietly, leaving the parade ground at quick march. When no officer is present the saluting is dispensed with.

CHAPTER II

Weapons

NO WEAPON is better than the skill of its user, and for this reason even inferior arms, when properly handled, can bring victory. Never despise the equipment with which you are fitted. Learn to make the most of it. No matter how excellent the armament a fighter possesses he can only gain superiority by continual practice.

If a man is armed only with a knife he can still beat another armed with a revolver. But he must know how to use that knife to the best advantage, to throw it with speed and accuracy from almost any position.

So, with all weapons, the rule is practice, practice, and still more practice.

In common with the infantryman of the Regular Army, the Home Guardsman is now equipped with the rifle as the main weapon for offence and defence. The early issue of shot guns is being withdrawn, but as later chapters will show, these sporting arms can be very effective.

The main features of the rifle are accuracy combined with handiness, and this combination has led to its acceptance in all armies as the chief item of personal armament. Five types are in general use for the Home Guard.

Many units have the standard Army rifle, the Short Magazine Lee-Enfield, widely known as the S.M.L.E. This is the handiest Service rifle ever made, although it is rather inaccurate at close range owing to the short " sighting base," i.e. the distance between the fore and back sights.

Large numbers of the Canadian Ross rifle are in circulation. This is a very accurate gun, its sighting base is nearly fourteen inches longer than on the S.M.L.E., and it has a simple pull-push bolt action which makes it useful for sniping work where movement must be kept to a minimum. Owing to its length it is rather unwieldy and needs much practice to obtain the best possible results.

An American rifle, the Pattern '17, is just coming into use. It is exactly similar to another rifle of American manufacture, the Pattern '14, which is the equipment of a number of Home Guard battalions. Both have an aperture back sight—which is the simplest form of sight for a Service rifle, and both have a Mauser type action—which is easier to produce than that of the S.M.L.E. But whereas the P.'14 type takes the ·303 British Service Cartridge, the P.'17 is bored for the ·300 American Cartridge. Special supplies of ammunition are therefore necessary, and the greatest care will be required to prevent the two types of ammunition being mixed. In the excitement of action this can easily happen and all ranks must take every precaution against such a disaster.

A few units have the No. 1 Mark IV rifle. This has an aperture back sight and a bolt action similar to the S.M.L.E. It is very accurate and uses the ·303 ammunition. Supplies of this type are limited at the present time but may be available in greater quantities later.

The first essential factor in the use of any of these weapons is the ability to judge distances. Fortunately practice in this can be obtained at any time and in any place. Every rifleman must train his sight in this respect. In town or country a simple exercise is always at hand. Choose two points, estimate the distance between them and then either pace out that distance or measure it on a large scale map, if one is available. Every man should know the length of his normal pace; the Standard Army length is 120 paces to 100 yards.

It is useful to have in one's mind a fixed length, such as a cricket pitch or football field, and use this as a unit of measure, dividing the distance under observation into so many pitches. If not sufficiently acquainted with these sports fields concentrate on definite lengths such as 50 or 100 yards.

Practise first on level ground until quite expert at ranges up to 400 yards. Home Guard action is not likely to exceed this distance and will be more probably about 200 yards and less.

Next carry out similar exercises on rising ground. The lie of the land, and weather conditions also, will affect the estimation of range. It is generally found to be underestimated on sloping ground or when the light is strong as on sunny clear days or over snow covered ground. Over-estimation is frequent in dull light, when firing from the kneeling or prone positions, and when the view is bounded as in looking along a deep valley or avenue of trees.

When proficient in judging ranges it is time to concentrate on firing positions, and true concentration is called for. The various movements should be carried through smoothly and each position must be held comfortably.

Volunteers will find it difficult at first to hold the rifle steadily in the firing positions. New arm movements strain the muscles and no opportunity should be lost in exercising them by repeating, time and time again, the drill for the various positions. Obviously, the quicker one's movements in getting into position, the more effective will be one's fire power.

The four firing positions are: standing, kneeling, prone and sitting. When in action, the rifleman's first concern will be the need for effective cover. Not so much to keep out of harm's way, as to enable him to get within the closest safe range so that his fire power will be at a maximum. For this reason the standing position will probably be used least, unless the action is carried on from strong defensive posts. Warfare over open ground will favour the other three positions.

Particular attention should be paid to the prone position. When scouting one must be able to vanish from the enemy's sight. Practice carefully dropping from attention to prone. Transfer the rifle smoothly from the right to the left hand *at the point of balance* and push it forward as the body falls so that it is in the firing position immediately the manœuvre is complete. Repeat the movements from the walk, and later from the run. Vary this by dropping from a crouching run.

The sitting position is excellent when long spells of observation duty are necessary where medium height cover is available. It may be maintained for hours. On sloping ground, firing down the slope or at a target on a higher level, this position should be adopted.

Some form of rest should be chosen when firing from the standing or kneeling positions. But *do not* let the rifle touch the rest or the aim will be upset. The weight of the rifle must be taken by the arms and either the left elbow or wrist should be on the rest.

Aiming practice does not call for actual firing at the rifle range. All the necessary work can be done with an empty magazine.

Take a target card, or cut a square of white cardboard, mark a black bulls eye in the centre and pierce a small hole in the centre of the bull. Fix this card on a stick and stand it firmly in the ground at a convenient height for prone firing. Make certain that the rifle is unloaded. Take up a firing position so that the foresight is a foot or so from the card. Get an assistant to lie at the other side of the target so that he can look through the small hole and align the gun sights with the bull.

Raise the rifle to the shoulder and aim at the bull. Concentrate on these points: —

(1) Keep the tip of the blade of the foresight just under the centre of the bull, i.e. to show half the black circle above the blade tip.

(2) Focus the eye on the target and not on the foresight.

(3) With an aperture back sight do not consciously centre the foresight in the aperture. The eye does this automatically.

(4) Keep the sights upright. Inclining the back sight to one side deflects the bullet low in the direction of inclination.

(5) Keep the rifle butt pressed firmly into the shoulder.

Lower the rifle and take fresh aim. Repeat this several times. The man looking through the hole in the target will be able to correct any faults. When the aim is correct he will find the two gun sights in perfect line with his sighting hole in the card.

Now repeat the exercises but this time practise trigger pressure. Note: —

(1) Grip the small of the butt firmly with the thumb and three fingers.

(2) Hold the gun firmly into the shoulder.

(3) Restrain the breathing at the moment of firing.

(4) Keep the first joint of the forefinger on, and do not consciously give a pull to the trigger.

The assistant behind the target will note any movement of the rifle as the trigger is pressed. But be sure the rifle is not loaded.

The same method can be used to improve the speed of aiming, and of course can be applied to any other firing position.

In all positions, and at all times, the loading, aiming and firing must be carried out with the absolute minimum of movement. Nothing advertises one's presence so much as movement. When working the bolt keep the head and rifle perfectly still, while the right hand moves carefully and smoothly back and forward again.

Keep your eye on the target at all times. Get the picture of the target as seen through the gun sights fixed in the mind and excellent " grouping " is assured. It is not necessary to close the left eye when proficiency in aiming has been reached. In fact it is an advantage to have both eyes open to obtain a wider view of the target and to avoid surprise attacks from other directions.

It will be noted that the bayonet has not so far been mentioned. The omission is deliberate. The bayonet should be classed with the cutlass as a fighting weapon. It has been obsolete since the American Civil War, and the Home Guard cannot afford the time to learn the ceremonial steps associated with its use. Hand to hand fighting in these days means pistol or hand grenade, preferably the latter. Scouting and stalking are excepted from the foregoing. To be effective, yet undetected a knife is the best weapon on such missions, and with this in view, the bayonet fitted to the Ross rifle is a peer of its type. The short blade is excellently proportioned for knife work. Other types may be used for toasting and tin-opening !

Do not stop at proficiency on the ground. Practise firing positions from trees, lying full length along a branch or sitting in a fork ; and at all times when firing move as little as possible, to conceal your presence.

Make a friend of your rifle, an inseparable friend. Take it everywhere, handle it continuously, for only in this way can its full support be obtained.

Sporting guns are being withdrawn as the supplies of Service rifles increase. Nevertheless these weapons can be made extremely powerful for some phases of Home Guard work.

Normally a sporting gun will not harm a man seriously except at close range, owing to the spread of the pellets. If this is prevented a 12 bore will kill at 100 yards. The operations involved are well known in some quarters of the country, but are quite new to others. The process is simple. Remove the top of the cartridge and take out the pellets. Then pour in melted candlegrease and replace the shot. Top up with more candlegrease as the first charge cools, so that the solid block is flush with the end of the cartridge casing. Now nick the casing with a sharp knife all round the cartridge level with the wad, but do not cut into the latter. This gives a bullet which will remain in solid form until the target is hit, and most effective results are then obtained for anti-tank work.

Few members of the Home Guard are as yet issued with pistols, and little need be said of them. Only an expert can obtain good results at long range, and there is no time for extensive training. The pistol should, then, be treated as a weapon for point blank use, its main feature being speed of action. Practise for this end only, as preparation for defence when stumbling into an enemy on patrol, or meeting him unexpectedly on a corner. For this, there is one, and only one place for the revolver holster—on the thigh. It should be held with two straps around the leg, the lower one firm and the upper one loose so that the holster swings slightly forward in the direction of withdrawal as the pistol is brought into action. The best results are obtained if the trigger mechanism is removed and the weapon operated by " thumbing " the hammer. Support the pistol by a firm grip with three fingers around the butt, the first finger acting as a steady, pointing forward alongside the trigger guard.

The gigantic mêlée which will surely result from an invasion of this country must develop into a series of " all-in " close quarter fights in which the most effective weapon will be the hand grenade.

With a range up to 35 yards a good H.E. fragmentation grenade will inflict injuries over a radius of 100 yards if used on hard or stony ground. Another great advantage is that such bombs may be improvised and do not need elaborate machinery for their production. Dynamite or gelignite may be packed tightly in ordinary eight ounce tins and fired by a length of Bickford fuse coupled to a detonator embedded in the explosive. If good fragmentation is required a large size standard gas or water pipe coupling, say two-inch bore, will prove excellent, and standard end-plugs may be used to close the container. A great deal of information useful in the manufacture of grenades will be found in the *Encyclopædia Britannica* under the sections Ammunition, Bombs, Explosives, etc.

For use against troops the grenades should be about one pound total weight. Against lorries a larger size is necessary containing one pound weight of explosive. For anti-tank work about one and three quarter pounds of explosive is required giving a bomb of probably two pounds total weight.

When throwing bombs remember that the effective radius is greater than the range of the thrower. Consequently the bomber must be in a protected position, or at least must fall flat on the ground as the bomb leaves the hand.

Four methods of grenade throwing will be described:—

STANDING in a trench or behind high cover. (*See* fig. 3, top view).

Movement 1

Left foot forward, bend knee, bring both hands to left knee and light fuse.

Movement 2

Swing body from hips backward without moving the feet. Raise left arm with hand pointing to target. Right hand with grenade, backwards and downwards. The thumb should be touching the fuse, and when the flame is felt the bomb must be thrown. Alternatively if the length of fuse and rate of burning are known, the seconds may be counted off before throwing. Take care there is no obstruction behind the right arm to knock the bomb out of the hand.

Movement 3

Lob the grenade high in the air with an overarm throw, straightening the body at the same time. Continue the motion, falling full length on the ground to avoid the

Fig. 3

explosion, if throwing from ground level behind light cover such as bushes or trees.

KNEELING, right knee on ground, left foot forward, knee bent.

Movement 1

Bring hands to knee and light fuse.

Movement 2

As in standing position above.

Movement 3

As in standing position, but keep knee on ground, falling flat as before.

PRONE, advancing behind low cover. (*See* fig. 3, lower view.) Lie full length, slightly turned on to left side. Elbows wide apart and bent so that hands are under the chest. Move the elbows forward alternatively digging each into the ground in turn and pull the body forward. At the same time use the right leg as a piston, bending the knee to bring the foot forward, then digging in the foot and pushing in unison with the elbow movement. The left leg should trail straight out behind. On reaching the firing point:—

Movement 1

Bring both hands forward and light the fuse.

Movement 2

Stretch right arm back, turning on to the left side of the body, but keeping the legs slightly apart for control.

Movement 3

Overarm stroke lobbing the bomb into the air. Lie flat until after the explosion.

MONKEY CRAWL, advancing behind cover of medium height. The body is bent double with knees tucked into the chest. Both hands touch the ground to assist in balance. Progress is then made in a half-trot, half-gallop manner, and on reaching the firing point, the kneeling position is used.

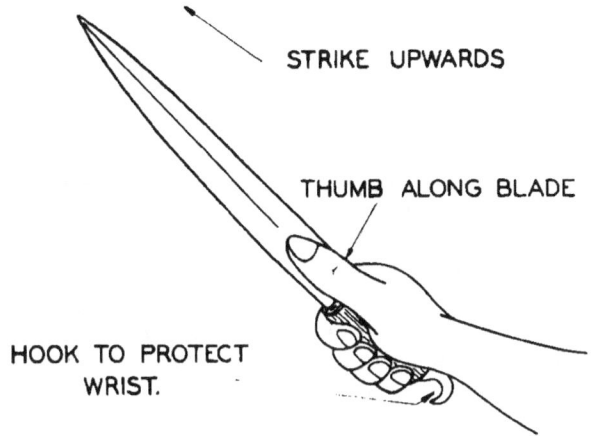

STRIKE UPWARDS

THUMB ALONG BLADE

HOOK TO PROTECT WRIST.

PATHAN KNIFE

FIG. 4

All attacks should be made cautiously. There is usually plenty of time, and the escape is made as soon as the explosion is over, taking advantage of the confusion following the attack. The line of escape should be well planned beforehand.

Some explanation must be given for the unusual recommendation of the knife as a weapon for organised troops. If the invasion develops there will be (as suggested in earlier pages) enormous opportunities for guerrilla warfare. Such operations have to be fully concealed to be effective and the use of firearms is bound to lead to detection.

The knife is silent in action, easily carried and easily concealed. When properly used its demoralising effect is tremendous. Not on those attacked, for they must be dealt with once and for all, but on comrades who are left wondering whose turn is next.

It is ideal for night work, against outposts, sentries, and small isolated units. When dealing with an outpost it should be possible to settle the sentry first and then dispose of six or seven men before they awake. This assumes good stalking and scouting ability.

Always attack a sentry from behind (*see* fig. 4). Place the left arm over his left shoulder, hand over his mouth to stop any warning shout. The knife must be inserted low down between the hip and the lowest rib and forced upwards. Left and right arm move simultaneously. Do not let the body slump noisily. The correct grip is with the thumb along the blade and the knife stroke should be upwards.

The Pathan knife as used on the North West frontier of India is an excellent type and a good version can be made from an infantry officer's sword. Cut off about 18 inches of the blade, and make two half-round sections of wood four inches long to form a handle. The blade length should be approximately $12\frac{1}{2}$ inches. Secure the pieces of wood, one each side of the blade, by two rivets passing right through wood and metal. Bind the handle to give a good finish. There is then 1½ inches of steel projecting below the handle and this must be ground to form a hook which will prevent the user being grasped round the wrist.

Superiority of armament is very largely a question of confidence in one's weapons. Eighteen inches of lead pipe or of light solid rubber tyre can be effective in the hands of a good stalker. A strong blow across the small of the back, in the lumbar region, will crumple an enemy without a sound.

These are drastic methods. To British minds they are definitely " not cricket." But we are not concerned with cricket. The task ahead is to rid the world of a curse— to rid the world of a force which will blot out our civilisation as quickly as the lead piping mentioned above will blot out an enemy. German methods are forcing us to admit that, in this war at least, " all is fair." The Home Guardsman must make up his mind that the purpose of his training is to kill the invader. Every shot with rifle or pistol must deplete the enemy forces. This is no time for kid gloves or half measures. And if rifle and pistol are inconvenient to the moment, alternative methods have been clearly given above.

So much for personal weapons. There is one group weapon which is issued to infantry sections and which the Home Guard must understand, the light machine gun, or Bren gun as it is popularly known.

This is usually operated by a section of nine men and all must be able to use it. In action a team of two is sufficient to work the gun. The remainder, who carry extra magazines for the automatic weapon, form a screen of riflemen who can add to the fire power of the section or protect the gun against attack from close quarters.

Of high accuracy, with a maximum rate of 120 rounds a minute, it gives valuable fire power to small units of infantry. The ability to simulate rifle fire by single rounds permits the concealment of the presence of an automatic weapon, and also saves ammunition until the maximum effect can be gained.

All machine guns should be sited to enfilade the target, that is, to give a field of fire along the length of the enemy position or across the direction of his advance. This is especially important with the L.M.G. (light machine gun) which does not spread the bursts to any great extent. Its accuracy does not permit of much error in sighting.

Bursts of five rounds each, about five times a minute, is the normal rate of automatic fire, except against aircraft. For the latter work a tripod mounting is used and bursts up to fifteen rounds each are advised. Rapid fire should be used with discretion to avoid overheating the barrel, which must be changed after firing ten consecutive magazines, i.e. 280 rounds.

It is vitally important during action to have ample supplies of ammunition available, and magazines must be refilled whenever a lull in fighting occurs.

The machine gun position must always be well supported by infantry. The enemy will concentrate on the destruction of such a strong point in the line, and will endeavour to outflank it and attack from the rear. To counteract this both flanks must be strongly guarded and alternative firing positions chosen in good time.

L.M.G.s should be used as the focal point of infantry action, assisting advancing troops by a covering fire. Their best targets are groups and close formations of the enemy, and they must always concentrate on enemy machine gun posts. The enemy should never be allowed to close within 500 yards of an L.M.G. as it is not suitable for close quarter fighting. The most effective range is 1,000 yards. When used in defensive action, L.M.G.s in neighbouring sections should be sited to give mutual support to one another.

CHAPTER III
Field Work

NO FIELD work should be built as a purely defensive point. It must always be considered as base *for an attack*. The site must therefore be one giving good covering fire for advancing infantry and favour concentrated fire to destroy enemy formations.

In an attack the infantry will rely on these positions to engage the enemy while they advance as quickly as possible. Infantry will not open fire during an advance unless the opposition is weak. But speed of advance is the main consideration. When setting up any fortified post avoid a point of the landscape which can be easily described such as any conspicuous landmark which could therefore be easily shelled. Arrange several points in depth to give mutual support and have a screen of infantry in front to locate enemy advances and to prevent flanking movements.

Concealment is vitally important in order to surprise any attack on the position. Alternative positions should be chosen in case concentrated fire is opened on the post. On locating a strong point the enemy infantry will halt until tanks or mortars are brought up. Tanks will at once start a flanking movement but mortars will immediately attack the position. The German mortar is a particularly efficient weapon of about 4 inch calibre. It forms part of the infantry organisation and can be dropped from aircraft in special containers. As an example of its use a case has been reported from France where a house was demolished at the first shot at 800 yards range. Such accuracy is the general standard of the German mortar batteries and the incident quoted is not an isolated case. The mortar, then, is definitely in the howitzer class.

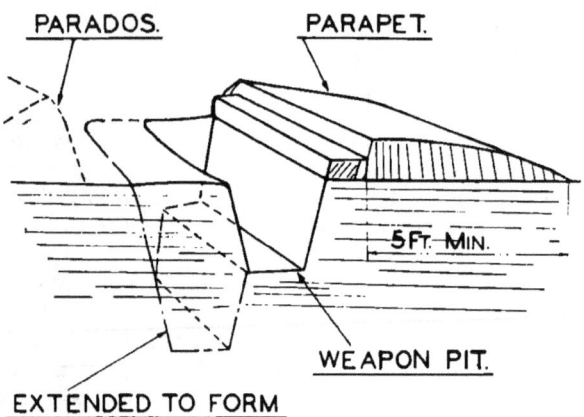
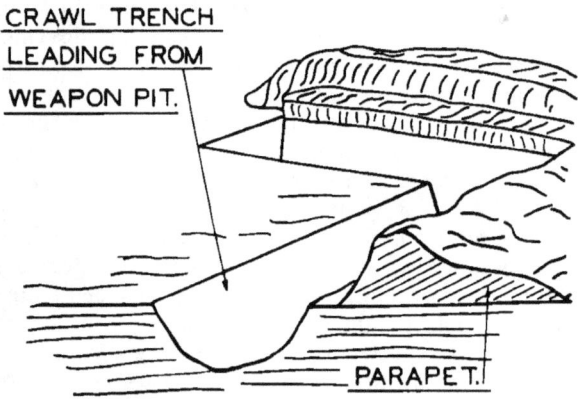

Fig. 5

Main defence lines should not be constructed on the forward slope of a hill as they could be easily shelled. Similarly, blockhouses erected on the crest of a hill will be demolished by mortar or artillery fire. An outpost position on the front slope can hold up infantry advancing across the valley, and should be connected by telephone to the main body established on the far side of the hill. When the enemy is strong enough to over-run the forward position the outpost must fall back if it has orders to do so and the main defence will deal with the attack as it comes over the crest.

A forward position, as just described, is expected to break up the enemy attack or to wear him down. Unless orders have been given to the contrary the defenders have to fight to the end. There is no exception to this rule.

The site of a field work must be carefully surveyed to reduce the area of dead ground and so prevent surprise attacks. " Dead ground " is any area which the defender cannot see from his firing position.

Every advantage must be taken of natural cover. Where digging has been in progress, the freshly turned earth shows up very clearly. Precautions are necessary to disguise this. If turf has been lifted it should be replaced on the parapets or front slopes of the post. Where vegetation is laid over the earth it must be renewed as it dries, and when fresh camouflage is placed it must be similar to that discarded or the fact will be noted by a keen observer. Cover should be made bullet proof and this calls for approximately 4 feet thickness of loose sand, two and a half feet of sand in bags, 5 feet of earth, 2 feet in brick walls, 8 feet of clay or only 1 foot of shingle.

The construction of field works means digging, and this is a task for the infantry man. It is no easy task but can be lightened by intelligent use of equipment. Once again practice is the cry. Many Home Guard units are taking part in tactical exercises. How many have been keen enough to dig weapon pits, trenches and bombing positions? The weapon pit requires four man hours' work. But it needs practice to do it in the time. Yet the ability to dig in quickly may mean success instead of failure in action. If only for personal safety, the Home Guardsman must learn the best way to use entrenching tools as soon as possible, and where to put his rifle and equipment so that they are not lost while digging.

A weapon pit is a trench 6 feet long, 3 feet 6 inches wide at the top, 2 feet wide at the bottom, and 3 feet deep. The top sod or earth is laid along the forward edge of the pit to form an elbow rest 18 inches wide and about 9 inches high. The remainder of the excavated earth is thrown forward to form an uneven parapet. This must be at least 18 inches high and 5 feet in forward thickness to be proof against bullets. If it is not 18 inches high the pit must be deepened to give a total cover of 4 feet 6 inches (*see* fig. 5).

When time permits weapon pits should be connected by crawl trenches. These are semi-circular troughs 3 feet 6 inches wide and about 18 inches deep. The excavated earth is thrown forward to form a rough parapet 18 inches high and 5 feet thick. The trenches should be planned so that they can be deepened later to form a proper trench system when coupled with the original weapon pits.

Useful practice could also be obtained during tactical exercises by occupying ditches as firing and bombing pits. Here again digging must be carried out to provide shelter from enfilade fire. At intervals cuttings should be made in the rear face at right angles to the line of the ditch. Such cuttings must extend beyond any hedgerow which may overhang the improvised trench. Excellent cover is then gained, behind which men can be withdrawn from one section to reinforce a weaker part of the line.

Digging often means night work and lying full length on the ground. The worst conditions must be tackled in practice before safety is assured.

Where traps are laid by the Home Guard be sure to advise the local Army Commanders, and advise in turn each Commander who comes to the area. Army units are changed so frequently that this precaution is essential.

In building an " asparagus line," a strong defence line of iron rails embedded in the ground, do not have the line continuous. While this would stop the enemy tanks it would also prevent our own armoured vehicles advancing. Where no tank traps are used the asparagus line should be perfectly camouflaged so that the tanks will be caught on the rails. But if land mines are available these should be laid across gaps in the line and the asparagus imperfectly camouflaged. This will induce the tanks on to the mined area. Tank drivers are a cautious clan and the Germans are masters at this trapping business.

At one point in Spain an asparagus line was built across country but had a gap at a large copse. The main line was quite well camouflaged but not quite so well as to be invisible to the tank crews. The drivers made for the copse which promised easy passage. The whole scheme, including the imperfect camouflage of the asparagus beds was a decoy trap to force the enemy into the real danger area. The area was mined and the tanks were destroyed.

CHAPTER IV

Street Fighting

AN INTIMATE knowledge of the town is essential and suitable exits must be arranged beforehand. If the action is defensive choose the site of the battle to your own advantage.

A good permanent barricade comprises two walls 8 feet high and 6 feet apart. The space between should be filled with heavy ballast. Barricades should be staggered and each just more than half the width of the road. When necessary the gap should be closed by pushing cars or lorries into it, removing the wheels and filling the bodies with ballast. A barricade must be strong enough to withstand mortar fire if its position has to be held for any length of time.

Supporting fire must be carefully arranged. Corner houses are ideal for blockhouses. Use the ground floor. In the room at the street corner build two walls and a roof to form a box within the room (*see* fig. 6). This is a safety measure against artillery or mortar fire. Do not use the windows, pack these with sandbags and knock loopholes in the walls. Make these at different levels so that the attackers cannot see the defenders moving from one position to another.

Make entrance to all houses as difficult as possible. Barricade doors and windows. All doorways should be covered by firing positions in adjoining houses.

With modern portable mortars the use of any but ground floor rooms is dangerous. If, however, only infantry are being opposed without stronger support, the upper floors may be used. Where possible fire from behind the wall facing the window, and not from the window itself. Knock

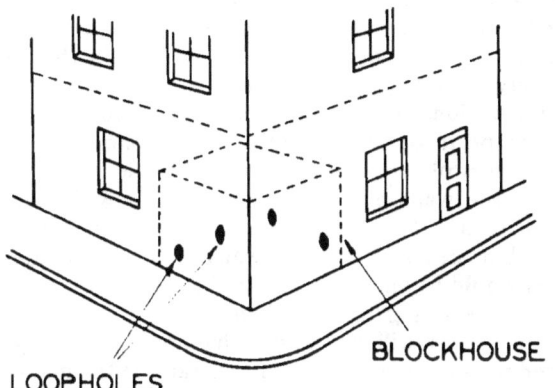

Fig. 6

LOOPHOLES   BLOCKHOUSE

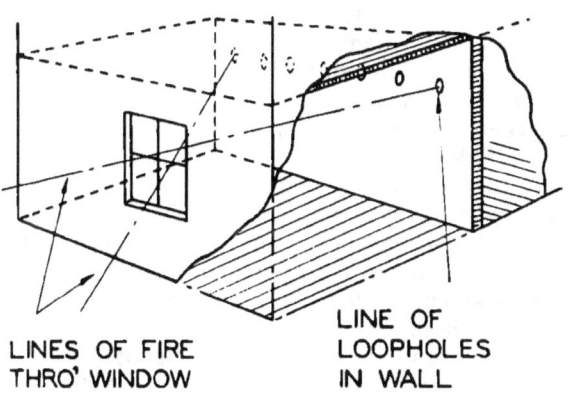

LINES OF FIRE THRO' WINDOW

LINE OF LOOPHOLES IN WALL

Fig. 7

several holes in the wall so that alternative firing points are available and also to give a good field of view (*see* fig. 7). When operating in this way from an adjoining room see that doors and windows at your rear are well blocked. If fighting from the room actually overlooking the street keep the muzzle of the rifle within the room. A rifle projecting through a wall is easily spotted.

If preparations are made well in advance, adequate loopholes can be made in the walls. These should take the form of steel plates with a central loophole hung on the inside of the walls and the loophole faced with brick to camouflage it. To ensure ease of communication holes may be knocked in the party walls of a row of houses, but this would be an advantage to the enemy if possession of one house was gained by them.

The attackers will be most vulnerable when they are grouped to enter a house. As a general rule the maximum fire from the houses will be from the side which is on the right of the enemy's advance. Right-handed riflemen will naturally work to the right of any cover as they are safer firing in a direction towards their left. The enemy will expect this and the advance will be along the right hand of the street. Left handed riflemen or well concealed loopholes on the opposite side of the street should have excellent targets and greatly strengthen the defence.

Street fighting is mainly close quarter work and the most formidable weapons for this are grenades or submachine guns. Large supplies of bombs should be available to the defenders. Unfortunately the supply of " Tommy " guns is very limited. Home Guardsmen should make every effort to obtain them from the enemy. To this end it should be noted that the tendency in firing these automatics is to aim high. If opposed to this gun get as low as possible and shoot quickly. When you have obtained the " Tommy " don't make the same mistake. Hold it horizontal and aim at the enemy's waist.

Avoid fighting from the roof if mortar fire is being used.

Fight from house to house whether advancing or withdrawing, never from one house to the next but one. If advancing be certain that each house is cleared of the enemy. If withdrawing make him earn every inch.

When advancing through a continuous line of houses such as a town street, gain the first, then knock a small hole in the party wall and quickly throw a grenade through. Knock a larger hole in the wall and throw in a handful of grenades. If there is no reply break down the wall and repeat as necessary.

Where there are gaps between the houses such as with semi-detached buildings, smoke bombs are very useful. As a substitute a handful of grenades may raise enough dust to cover the movement. The bombs should not be used only at the point of advance as a single disturbance will draw fire. Similar tactics should be carried out from several positions simultaneously to confuse the enemy.

An important factor in street fighting is to know whether the occupants of a house are friend or foe. A pre-arranged signal should be used, and it must be something inconspicuous so that the enemy will not spot and copy it. One suggestion is to fix a dirty handkerchief in one particular corner of a window.

CHAPTER V

Anti-tank Work

OPERATIONS against armoured fighting vehicles have two objectives:—

First: To destroy the tank, or if this fails

Second: To get the crew outside the tank.

Now tanks must be expected anywhere and from any direction. They work in small numbers, say two or three with an advance guard of motor cyclists. The range of action is large and the speed of the lighter types is about 40 mile an hour on good surfaces.

If used in the early phase of an invasion they will probably be of 8 to 10 tons weight. Heavy models could not be brought into action unless the Germans were in occupation of a suitable coast port. But the lighter types can be transported by air and are essential to enemy operations.

It can be safely stated that light tanks unsupported by infantry are easy prey as long as the roads are clear of refugees and provided everyone is prepared to fight them. Now that this country has been turned into an armed camp there will be no excuse if enemy tanks scouting in advance of the main body survive the first road block on their path.

The formation of tanks works with the motor cycle advance guard about a quarter of a mile ahead. Where these are halted the first tank stops and when that happens the second tank which will be about 75 or 100 yards astern also stops, and so on down the line. If the motor cyclists are attacked by a force stronger than the armoured vehicles, these will turn and retreat.

It is important, then, that the units on anti-tank work should let the advance party pass. Suitable reception for them will have been arranged farther along the road and out of sight of the main quarry.

A tank trap should be sited where no alternative route is available for the vehicle. Tank drivers always take the line of least resistance and will turn off a road on the open country if a road block can be avoided in that way. Thick woods or a lake bordering the road, or very substantial buildings are excellent for the purpose, and a deep cutting with steep sides will also serve. If the road is too narrow to allow the tank to turn so much the better. Above all, the trap should be around a bend where the tank will come on it unexpectedly.

Tanks do not charge obstacles as the impact would injure the crew. The vehicle approaches quickly, then slows down, noses up to the block and attempts to push its way through or climb over. During the time that the tank is slowed down or temporarily stopped the attack should be made. The safest offensive position is close to the tank. Its guns cannot be depressed more than 25 degrees from the horizontal and the turrets do not turn at high speed. A determined man rushing from cover at the roadside, can get to the side of the tank and fire a bullet through the slot in the driver's visor. A single shot in this manner has been known to kill an entire crew by ricochetting from the steel sides. Latest models of the German tanks have a row of holes in the plating instead of a visor for the drivers, and buck shot is then more effective than a single bullet. Refer to Chapter II for instructions on the adaptation of sporting cartridges for this work.

Another factor in favour of the attack is that tank crews lead a very hard life in action. If the hatches of the vehicle are kept closed, the endurance of the crew is about four hours, and they will nearly always be in a " jittery " state and easily rushed into making a fatal mistake.

First arrange a motor-cycle trap. This is formed by

stretching a strong wire across the road from trees or substantial posts. Put it about 4 feet or 4 feet 6 inches above ground. The single wire may be supplemented at intervals with a coil of barbed wire and further on by the " knife rest " device comprising two wood crosses on the ends of a long pole with barbed wire wound over the resulting structure. These should be sited some distance beyond the bend in the road at which the real tank trap is laid, but in full view from that point. A system of signals is necessary so that warning of the approach of the enemy may be sent back from a look-out post to the tank trap and on to the motor cycle trap. The men operating the latter should have suitable trenches or cover in which to hide when the wires have been drawn into position. From their positions they must be ready to attack any riders who are merely thrown from the machines and not incapacitated.

On rounding the bend and finding the advance unit in difficulties the tank will stop. As soon as it begins to slow down the main attack should begin. From a bombing trench at the roadside (*see* fig. 8), suitably camouflaged and protected, high explosive bombs must be thrown and these should be aimed at the track and sprockets to destroy the driving mechanism. A single bomber is enough and he should throw one bomb as the tank approaches the trench, dodging back under cover to avoid the explosion, and a second as it passes, again dodging back to safety.

In case this attack fails a series of rifle pits on the opposite side of the road are brought into action. From these are thrown incendiary bombs of the type popularly called " Molotoff cocktails." They are aimed at the bogie wheels which support the tank's driving track. As these bogie wheels are rubber tyred and the links and bearings nearby are always surrounded by quantities of grease, it is quite easy to start a good fire when the Molotoff breaks. Immediately a hit is registered the bomb throwers feed the fire with a quick succession of the incendiaries.

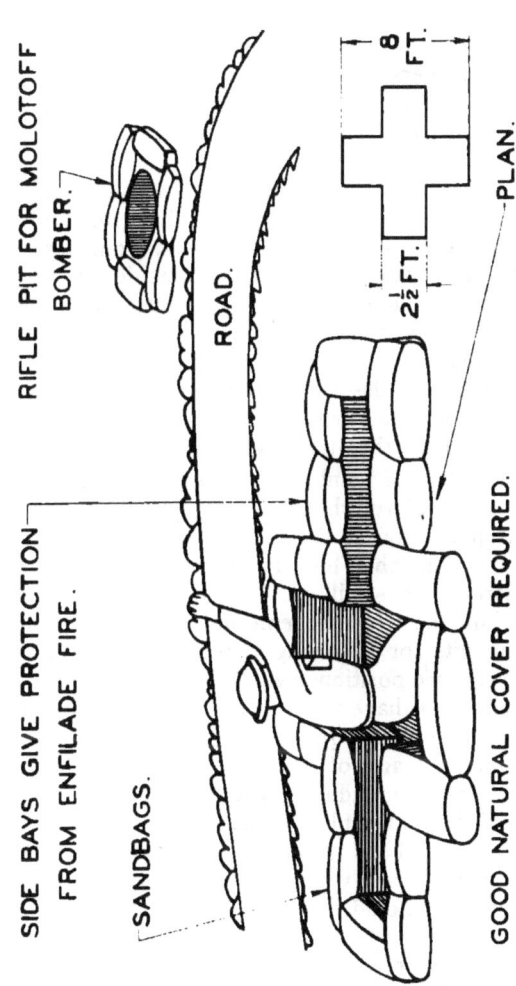

Fig. 8

This action brings out the tank crew, and the supporting infantry must be well placed around the trap to deal with them. As soon as the hatch opens, be prepared for hand grenades thrown from inside the tank. From sheltered posts snipers should be able to pick off the crew as they scramble out. They are not likely to be in the best fighting spirit if the bombers have done their work properly.

When the original H.E. bomb attack is successful it may still be necessary to use the incendiary method to bring out the crew. Remember that hand grenades and small bombs are useless against the outside of tanks. They are valuable, however, if lobbed into the vehicle once the hatch is open, and this precaution must always be taken to ensure that all the crew are accounted for. Anti-tank bombs, as described in Chapter II, must be about two pounds total weight.

To deal with any other tanks which may be following the first, the system of bombing pits must be arranged in series at intervals of roughly 80 to 100 yards. The rear tanks will stop as soon as they suspect that the leader is in trouble, and must then be attacked immediately.

Where there is a possibility of tanks approaching from either direction, the whole scheme must be duplicated so that bombing pits for following tanks and the wire trap for motor cycles are positioned each side of the main trap. The latter will then have to be placed right on the bend unless sufficient men and equipment are available for main attacks around each arm of the road.

Another method for inducing the leading tank to slow up is to build a dummy blockhouse on the bend. Have this well camouflaged and manned by a few men. As soon as fire is opened the tank will slow up to locate the sudden attack. Bombing should begin as soon as the vehicle is within range.

Land mines may be added to the power of the trap, and should be laid in lines across the road, at intervals of about

10 yards. There will then be no fear of the tank using part of the road which is not mined. Where the mines are improvised, say of dynamite or gelignite, they may be detonated with a very simple circuit. Take a 2½ volt pocket lamp bulb. Rub a hole in the glass with emery paper and solder contact wires to the central terminal and to the screwed metal boss. Fill the bulb with gunpowder and wrap a piece of cloth over it to keep the powder in. If a 6 volt dry battery is connected to the contacts an excellent detonator is obtained.

If an ample supply of land mines is at hand, they could be used as the main attack, replacing the H.E. bomber and his trench. The Molotoff bombers should be kept together on one side of the road to ensure the maximum concentration. Have plenty of Molotoff bombs to gain the best results. As soon as the first hits, the fire must be spread with all speed.

Some Home Guard units have experimented with flame throwers. Two methods have been tried and the scheme is worthy of development. A jet of paraffin is used, and in one scheme this is thrown by an ordinary stirrup pump. In the second arrangement a car foot pump delivers air at 40 pounds per square inch pressure to a drum containing the paraffin and forces the liquid out through the jet. Ignition is made by throwing a grenade at the target and a liberal quantity of the fluid must be splashed around before the bomb is thrown.

Flame throwers must be used at close range as the jet atomises quickly and the tip of the flame is not very hot. They would be useful at road blocks where the tank is brought to a standstill.

This raises the question of flame-throwing tanks. These would only be met with if the invasion succeeded as far as the capture of a port. They may be recognised by the 20 foot nozzle which projects forward and by the fuel trailer at the rear. The jet has a range of 100 yards, but cannot be trained from side to side. The fuel trailer is a vulnerable point and should be an easy target for Home Guard units.

If barricades are used they should be substantial and of the type described in Chapter IV. Anti-tank pits are of no use if less than 12 feet deep. The sides must be steep enough to prevent the tracks gripping and solid enough to stop the tracks digging the surface away until the slope is easy to climb. In all cases they must be built where *no alternative route is possible*.

While dealing with tanks it is interesting to note the light armoured vehicles now being issued to Home Guard units. These have no roof, and are therefore very vulnerable to grenade attacks. A stout wood or steel cover should be improvised if these cars are to be used seriously.

CHAPTER VI
Anti-Aircraft

THE Home Guard has registered its first kill, and all honour is due to the unit concerned. The incident proves what determination and cool judgment can accomplish and should spread confidence throughout the whole organisation.

Parachute and air-borne troops will be the special prey of the Home Guard. It must be fully appreciated that troop landings may be carried out at a large number of points in this country. Aerodromes are not essential. Most golf courses, for instance, are admirable for this purpose and large fields which are not masked by tall trees give ample opportunities for safe landings.

Many of these areas have been protected by digging trenches or setting heaps of earth over the area. Two conditions of landing must however be catered for. If the Germans wish to land a large number of troops they will have to fly the aeroplanes off when the soldiers have disembarked. The landings will then be normal ones, with the undercarriage wheels extended. To prevent this, trenches are advised or alternatively wire ropes stretched from strong posts at intervals over the ground and about 4 feet above it. Trenches should be 3 feet 6 inches to 4 feet minimum width and at least 3 feet deep to trap the large wheels of modern aircraft. But if a company of picked men has to be landed for special demolition work, the enemy will not trouble about the safe return of the aircraft. Most modern planes have retractable landing gear, and there is little danger to the occupants when a machine lands with the wheels up. It cannot be flown away again as the propellers are always damaged badly. With the large

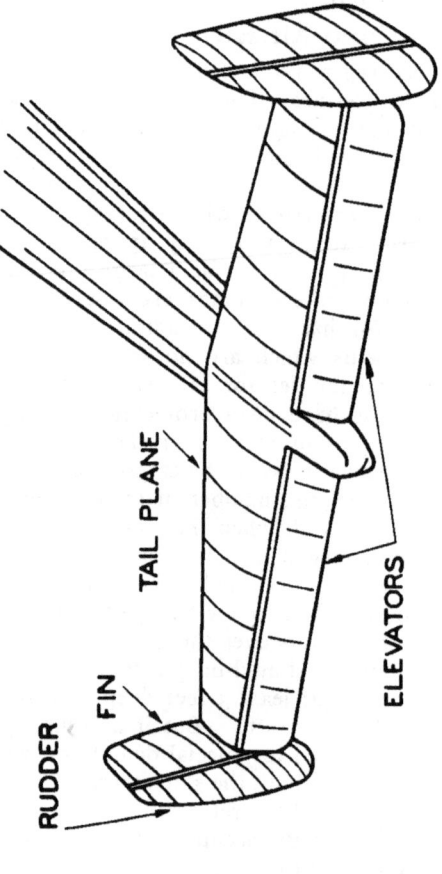

AIRCRAFT TAIL UNIT.

FIG. 9

machines now in use trenches will not prevent such landings, and the mounds of earth so often seen are also insufficient.

Solid obstructions such as tree stumps or their equivalent are necessary, so that the under surface of the aeroplane fuselage will be ripped open.

If an enemy machine is encountered on the ground the easiest way to disable it is to damage the elevator (*see* fig. 9). The butt end of a rifle will smash the light structure of these components, and there is no need to try to burn the aircraft. Actually the Home Guard should make every endeavour to prevent the destruction of aircraft and should not hesitate to shoot the crew of an enemy plane when they attempt to set it on fire. The undamaged machine gives valuable technical information and can also be used against its former owners—a very satisfying thought.

Rifle fire against aircraft is effective up to 3,000 feet altitude, but mass firing must be resorted to. Due allowance must be made for the high speed of the machine, and the rifle must be aimed well ahead of the target. The L.M.G. is excellent for this work, and the space forward of the aircraft should be peppered with bullets. There is then more chance of the plane flying into a bullet and so disabling the pilot. An Italian mathematical analysis of small arms anti-aircraft fire estimates that one bullet in 450 will hit a machine. Rapid fire is certainly necessary.

Excellent identification charts are now available, and these should be studied so that recognition is immediate and also to prevent attack on friendly aeroplanes.

APPENDIX

Message Writing

ADOPT the army system and keep the message short but clear. Important messages should be sent in two ways, by different routes. At the head of the message give first the address to which it is sent, next the address from which it comes. When dealing with military authorities simply address to the Battalion and Company concerned. Omit reference to the C.O. Next give three groups of data, first on the left, initials of the sender and the serial number of the message for the day, e.g. if it is the fifth sent that day the group would read X.Y.5. Avoid dashes or strokes. The middle group gives the number of the day of the month, e.g. for August 21, simply the number 21. The right hand group denotes a message replying to one received previously and gives the initials and serial number of this, i.e. it repeats the information in the left hand group of the message which is being answered. Then follows the message as concisely as possible. It is a good tip to imagine your message will cost *you* a pound a word. If a full stop is needed in the text it is shown by a dot in the middle of a circle. Do not put a full stop at the end of a message.

Next comes the signature, followed by rank of the sender and then his appointment. In the bottom right hand corner give the time of despatch in 24-hour clock code (in which there is no midnight, but either 23·59 hours or 00·01 hours). Finally in the bottom left hand corner give the method of despatch.

If an acknowledgment is required write the code ACK in block letters at the end of the message. Do not abbreviate for fear of a misunderstanding. Only fully trained people should use standard forms of abbreviation, and even then mistakes arise. When referring to points of the compass write them in full and block letters, e.g. NORTH or SOUTH WEST.

www.ingramcontent.com/pod-product-compliance
Lightning Source LLC
Chambersburg PA
CBHW060221050426
42446CB00013B/3128